Atlantic Puffin

Snail Kite

Waldrapp Ibis

Peregrine Falcon

Philippine Eagle

Europe

Asia

Micronesian Kingfisher

Guam Rail

Black Palm Cockatoo

Africa

Australia

Bali Mynah

Wood Stork

Shoebill Stork

Harpy Eagle

Mauritius Kestrel

Black-footed Penguin

SAVING ENDANGERED BIRDS

ENSURING A FUTURE IN THE WILD

BY THANE MAYNARD

A Cincinnati Zoo Book

FRANKLIN WATTS

New York • Chicago • London • Toronto • Sydney

This b[ook] ... [wh]o has studied
and pho[tographed] ... [libr]ary, and whose
ph[otographs] ... [im]possible.

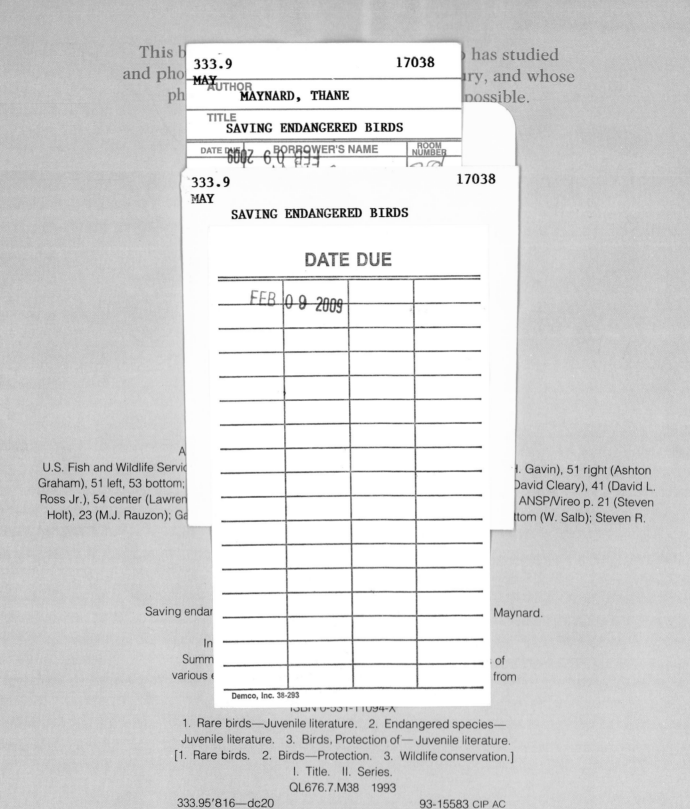

A[cknowledgments]
U.S. Fish and Wildlife Servic[e] ... [H]. Gavin), 51 right (Ashton Graham), 51 left, 53 bottom; ... David Cleary), 41 (David L. Ross Jr.), 54 center (Lawren[ce] ... ANSP/Vireo p. 21 (Steven Holt), 23 (M.J. Rauzon); Ga[vin] ... [bo]ttom (W. Salb); Steven R.

Saving endan[gered birds] ... Maynard.

In[cludes] ...
Summ[ary] ... [lif]e of
various e[ndangered] ... from

ISBN 0-531-11094-X

1. Rare birds—Juvenile literature. 2. Endangered species—
Juvenile literature. 3. Birds, Protection of—Juvenile literature.
[1. Rare birds. 2. Birds—Protection. 3. Wildlife conservation.]
I. Title. II. Series.
QL676.7.M38 1993
333.95'816—dc20   93-15583 CIP AC

WHAT MAKES BIRDS SPECIAL?

Birds are the most showy, noisy, brightly colored, and cocky animals in the world. There are about 9,000 species of birds worldwide, and they all lay eggs. But lots of other animals lay eggs, too. And it's not wings that make birds different, since bats and bugs have great wings. It's *feathers* that make a bird a bird.

Scientists believe that birds evolved from small dinosaurs. For years it was thought that the first animal ever to wear feathers, and the very first bird, was *Archaeopteryx*, an animal with bird-like characteristics that lived some 140 million years ago, during the Jurassic period. However, recent fossil discoveries have shown that crow-sized ancestors of birds may have existed 75 million years before that time.

WHAT WILL IT TAKE TO SAVE ENDANGERED BIRDS?

- **Identifying and protecting each bird's habitat**—the type of area it needs to live—is the most important step in saving endangered birds.

- **Protecting wetlands** around the world from the pressure of human development.

- **Research** into the behavior and migration of birds is essential for future conservation efforts.

- **Ending trade in wild-caught birds**. Every year thousands of birds are taken from the wild and sold as pets.

- **Breeding wild birds in captivity**. Captive breeding has helped save some species, such as California condors and Mauritius kestrels, from extinction, and they now fly free in the wild again.

- **Supporting environmental and wildlife laws**, such as the Endangered Species Act and the Wild Bird Conservation Act, that protect wild creatures.

LEARNING ABOUT BIRDS

Nearly everywhere we go, we see more birds than all other animals combined. This is partly because birds can fly, and thus escape their predators—most of the time.

Birds are all around us, and so are bird *watchers*. To learn about birds, you don't have to travel to the plains of Africa or the rain forests of South America. Local birding clubs or an Audubon Society will help you get started. With a pair of binoculars and a field guide to the birds, you're ready to go. All it takes to learn about birds is to walk outside and start looking around. A world of birds waits in every backyard.

"WILD BIRDS ARE ONLY 2 PERCENT FEATHER AND BONE, AND 98 PERCENT PLACE."

**—David Brower,
former president of the Sierra Club**

As you read about the birds in this book, think about where they live: the trees they perch in, the cliffs they nest upon, and the open fields where they hunt. It is habitat that shapes the bird, not the other way around. This wild setting is vital if we are to save our wild species.

Atlantic Puffin

Fratercula arctica

Range: Atlantic coast, northern Maine to Canada,
northern Europe, Greenland, Iceland
Habitat: Coastal and offshore waters
Diet: Fish and marine invertebrates
Size: 12 in. (30 cm) long
Reproduction: One egg per clutch; incubation:
39–45 days
Threats: Human intrusion and poaching

These little birds with clownlike appearance are among the most appealing birds in the world. Their brightly colored bills serve a number of purposes. The bill is very strong and well adapted to catching fish. It also serves as a shovel when the birds dig out crevices in which to nest. It takes five years for the bill to develop its full adult color which is a sign that the bird is sexually mature.

Puffins are a little like northern versions of penguins. They roost on rocky coasts and islands of the North Atlantic Ocean and hunt fish in shallow water. But puffins, unlike penguins, can fly. Their wings are smaller in relation to their body weight than is true for most birds, so they are not great long-distance flyers. Still, puffins get around well and fly low over the ocean to catch small fish.

Atlantic puffins are slow breeders, typically raising only one young every few years. To keep the egg warm, the adult holds it with one wing against an area of skin under the wing called the "brood patch." Both parents share in **incubation** and tending the young puffins after hatching.

Puffins were completely gone from the Atlantic coast of the United States for more than 100 years, slaughtered by hunters in the eighteenth and nineteenth centuries. They were easily killed since they had few predators, and therefore few defenses; and they are curious, slow-moving birds. Sailors could walk right up and hit them over the head.

Today the Atlantic puffin is making a comeback. Dr. Steven Kress of Cornell University has been reintroducing puffins to Eastern Egg Rock, off the Maine coast, since the 1970s. The island's population is now at 40 pairs of puffins, and climbing. And the number of people interested in saving the Atlantic puffin is growing as well. From late spring to early fall, tour boats take visitors out near Eastern Egg Rock to hunt puffins, using only cameras and binoculars to "capture" their prey.

Attwater's Prairie Chicken

Tympanchus cupido attwateri

Range: Texas
Habitat: Coastal prairie
Diet: Plants, insects
Size: 17–18 in. (42.5–45 cm) long
Reproduction: Average clutch: 2 eggs; incubation: 23–24 days
Threats: Agricultural and residential development

Not all chickens are in the supermarket. Some live in the wilds of Texas. Attwater's prairie chicken, a dark **subspecies** of the greater prairie chicken, is noted for orange skin patches on the sides of the male's neck. These inflate and become prominent during **courtship** when the male bird emits low, booming calls as it struts around, hoping to attract a mate.

Prairie chickens, as the name suggests, nest in tall prairie grasses that provide cover and food for the birds. After mating, male prairie chickens do not help to take care of the young. The female lays a **clutch** of a dozen eggs, incubates them for 24 days until they hatch, and then feeds the young for a week to 10 days, until **fledging** occurs. Prairie chickens are ground feeders; they peck for plants, seeds, and insects.

The spread of cities, conversion of habitat for agriculture and oil and gas development, and human population growth in Texas are crowding out the prairie chicken. Today there may be fewer than 900 Attwater's prairie chickens, down from about 8,700 in 1940 and from more than 1 million in the nineteenth century. In the early 1960s the World Wildlife Fund took action to reverse this trend, purchasing prairie chicken habitat in southern Texas. In 1972 the U.S. Fish and Wildlife Service put this land together with additional donated lands to create the Attwater's Prairie Chicken National Wildlife Refuge, several thousand acres of protected native prairie in southeast Texas. For the species to be saved, conservationists will have to protect more prairie habitat and establish a captive-breeding program to produce additional birds to release in wildlife refuges.

Bald Eagle

Haliaeetus leucocephalus

Range: Strongholds in western Canada and Alaska, sparsely distributed over the lower 48 states
Habitat: Coasts, rivers, large lakes
Diet: Primarily fish, sometimes carrion, less often rabbits, squirrels, waterfowl
Size: 30–43 in. (75–107.5 cm) long
Reproduction: Average clutch: 2 eggs; incubation: 34–36 days
Threats: Pollution, pesticides, shooting, human encroachment

Bald eagles are large, beautiful birds of prey, with a wingspan up to 8 feet (2.4 m) across. Adult eagles have black-brown bodies, white heads and tails, and yellow beaks and legs. Bald eagles are not really bald. Their heads, like their tails, are covered with snow-white feathers, but this white plumage does not develop until the bird's fourth year. It is a sign of maturity, and may help to attract mates. During their first few years, young eagles are brown with mottled white wings, and resemble golden eagles. Eagles mate for life, and both parents share in the incubation and rearing of the young. Adopted as the United States' national symbol in 1782 for their fierce and independent image, bald eagles in truth are timid creatures.

The hooked beak and sharp **talons**, as on all birds of prey, are used for catching and killing prey. Bald eagles are opportunistic, which means they adapt their feeding habits to the available food supply. They feed on fish, which they scoop from the surface of the water and carry off to eat on land or while perched in a tree. They also catch rodents and other small mammals and feed on **carrion**.

A male and a female eagle together build a nest high in a tree near open water. The eagles' stick nests are among the largest in the world, and some are used for many years. Nests 12 feet (3.6 m) high, 9 feet (2.7 m) across, and weighing more than 1 ton (.9 tonne) have been seen.

Habitat loss and pollution that affects their reproduction still threaten the species. However, since the pesticide **DDT** was banned in the 1960s, the bald eagle population has increased. It is believed that 30,000 eagles live in Alaska; nearly that number nest in Canada. About 2,500 nesting pairs of eagles live in the lower 48 states, with most in the Pacific Northwest, Florida, the Upper Great Lakes, and Chesapeake Bay.

Black-Footed Penguin

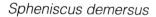

Spheniscus demersus

Range: Southern Africa—Namibia to Mozambique
Habitat: Coastal and offshore waters
Diet: Fish
Size: Up to 25 in. (62.5 cm) high
Reproduction: Average clutch: 1 egg
Threats: Egg and guano harvesting, coastal development, oil pollution, and commercial fishing

Also known as the "jackass penguin" for its raucous call that resembles a donkey's bray, the black-footed penguin is a medium-size penguin that lives in colonies on coastal islands of southern Africa.

Like other penguins of the genus *Spheniscus*, the black-footed penguin has black plumage on its head and back and white on its front, and a broad black stripe along its sides. Its face is black and white, and the flippers are black. Closely related species are the Magellanic penguin and the Galápagos penguin, both of which range along the western coast of South America.

All penguins are good swimmers, with wings that serve as powerful flippers. Black-footed penguins catch small fish, and during nesting season, both parents bring the fish to feed to their young. They live and nest in groups.

Millions of black-footed penguins once lived in their current range. However, as early as 1844, they were declining rapidly. Penguin dung, or guano, was actively collected for fertilizer, and the birds' eggs were often smashed and young birds killed in the process. From the late 1800s until the 1930s, the birds also were disturbed by egg hunters, who collected over 500,000 eggs each year.

Penguin-egg collecting was banned by an international treaty in 1969, and other fertilizers are used instead of guano. However, the population continues to decline, indirectly hurt by oil spills, harbor development, and overfishing within its waters. Research is under way to learn how to help the penguins.

Black Palm Cockatoo

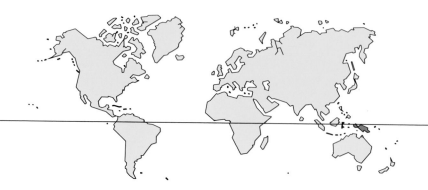

Probosciger aterrimus

Range: New Guinea
Habitat: Scrubland and open forest
Diet: Fruits, seeds, and insects
Size: 30 in. (75 cm) long
Reproduction: Average clutch: 2–5 eggs; incubation: 48 days
Threats: Pet trade and habitat destruction

There are 327 species of psittacines, or members of the parrot family. One of the rarest is the black palm cockatoo, which makes its nest in cavities within the trunks of palm trees. This beautiful black bird is among the largest of the cockatoos, and it shares the dramatic cockatoo habit of raising its crest feathers when alarmed. It is native to scrub and forest areas of New Guinea.

All 16 species of cockatoos are principally vegetarians, feeding on fruits, seeds, and nuts. The black palm cockatoo, with its massive bill, can break open the very thick shelled fruits of various tropical palms. Human beings usually need an ax. It is probably from this food source that the species gets its name. The bird also feeds on insect larvae it extracts from rotten wood.

After the female lays a clutch of two to five eggs within the nest cavity, both parents share in incubating the eggs and feeding the young birds for about two months.

Black palm cockatoos are most active in the middle of the day, congregating in large flocks to forage for food.

Unfortunately, the black palm cockatoo has been hurt both by deforestation of its native range and by overcollecting for the pet trade. Long favored by parrot owners, today there are very few of this magnificent species left flying in the wild.

Brown Pelican

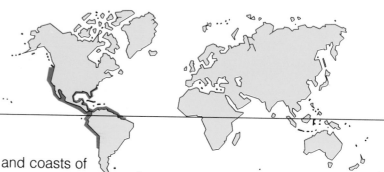

Pelecanus occidentalis

Range: Atlantic and Gulf coasts, California, and coasts of South America
Habitat: Salt bays, beaches, and coastal islands
Diet: Fish
Size: 50 in. (125 cm) long
Reproduction: Average clutch: 3 eggs; incubation: 28–30 days
Threats: Pesticides and habitat loss

Brown pelicans are large fish-eating birds with wingspans up to 7 feet (2.1 m) across. They are noted for their scooplike bills, which open and serve as nets when the pelicans plunge headfirst into the ocean to catch fish. Pelicans are good flyers, able to glide along over the wave tops to search for prey. The brown pelican gets its name from its light brown body and the dark brown plumage on its neck during the early spring and summer breeding season.

Brown pelicans nest in large colonies on low coastal islands. They prefer mangrove trees for their nests, although they also use cedar, oak, seagrape, and other trees that grow just beyond high-tide level. Colonies sometimes total over 400 pelicans. The male and female help incubate the three eggs. Pelicans are **altricial** nesters, which means their young are hatched featherless and defenseless. Down feathers appear after about ten days but the birds are not ready to fledge until they are about three months old.

Heavy spraying with pesticides such as **DDT** during the 1950s and 1960s nearly killed off the brown pelican. The chemicals created two problems for the birds, directly poisoning adult pelicans and interrupting the breeding cycle. DDT reduces the formation of calcium in the bird's eggs. The eggshells become so thin that they break during incubation. Fortunately, in 1972 the U.S. Environmental Protection Agency banned the use of DDT, and the brown pelican is recovering.

Nearly 12,000 pairs of brown pelicans now nest in Florida. In Louisiana, the bird was extinct in the wild 20 years ago. Today about 1,000 breeding pairs reside there, thanks to reestablishment by the U.S. Fish and Wildlife Service with pelicans from the Florida population. The California population is nearly 100,000 birds.

California Condor

Gymnogyps californianus

Range: Southern California
Habitat: Isolated rocky cliffs
Diet: Carrion
Size: 43–50 in. (107.5–125 cm) long
Reproduction: Average clutch: 1 egg; incubation:
42–50 days
Threats: Human encroachment, extremely low numbers

California condors are one of the biggest birds in North America, with wingspans over 9 feet (2.7 m). They are large vultures that, like all vultures, eat carrion, or dead animals. Historically, they fed on the bodies of wolves, hoofed animals, and even washed-up whales and seals.

Condors were once as close to the edge of extinction as a species can get. In 1987, there were only 27 birds left. So many people had crowded into southern California that there was no space left for the condors in the arid canyons of the Pacific Coast. So scientists began one of the most controversial wildlife rescue efforts in history.

In 1987 the U.S. Fish and Wildlife Service captured the remaining wild California condors and placed them in two zoos for captive breeding. Some critics believed that the zoos didn't know how to breed condors and feared the birds would never be released to the wild.

However, the U.S. Fish and Wildlife Service scientists, and those at the zoos, believed it would be a greater wrong to allow the species to dwindle into extinction. Fortunately, breeding condors was not as difficult as some people feared. After a few years the number of condors had doubled, and in January 1992 two California condors were released to the wild at the Sespe Condor Sanctuary, a federal wildlife preserve in the Los Padres National Forest.

Another cause of the decline of the California condor was lead poisoning from bullets and shotgun pellets left in dead animals killed by hunters. To protect the released condors, lead-free food is set out in Los Padres National Forest. Even though the birds can fly more than 100 miles (160 km) in a single flight, tests with their cousins, Andean condors, have shown that they return to easily available food when they are hungry.

Guam Rail

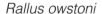

Rallus owstoni

Range: Endemic to Guam, extinct in the wild
Habitat: Open scrub forests and wetlands
Diet: Invertebrates, small animals, and plants
Size: 12–14 in. (30–35 cm) long
Reproduction: Average clutch: 2–4 eggs; incubation:
24–30 days
Threats: Introduced predator

Rails are medium-size marsh birds that inhabit open scrubland and wetland areas through most of the continents of the world. The Guam rail is native to the Micronesian island of Guam in the South Pacific Ocean.

Guam rails spend most of their time on the ground, searching for slugs, snails, insects, amphibians, flowers, and seeds on which to feed. They also nest on the ground, laying a clutch of two to four eggs, which are incubated for about a month.

Today the Guam rail is extinct in the wild. It was eaten out of existence by the poisonous brown tree snake, which was accidentally introduced to its island home in the 1940s. Natural predator–prey relationships do not lead to the extinction of a species because—over many generations—a balance is reached in which the hunter and the hunted actually depend on each other. However, when a predator is introduced, the prey is usually defenseless against it. The population can be decimated, as was the case for the Guam rail.

Through captive breeding programs that have been in progress since 1984, scientists hope to reestablish the Guam rail in its native home. Since 1990 experimental releases have been tried, with some success, on the island of Rota, off the coast of Guam. The birds cannot be returned to Guam itself until the brown tree snake is removed.

Harpy Eagle

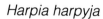

Harpia harpyja

Range: Central America and northern South America
Habitat: Tropical forests
Diet: Sloths, monkeys, smaller mammals, and birds
Size: 36–43 in. (90–107.5 cm) long
Reproduction: Average clutch: 2 eggs
Threats: Tropical deforestation

The harpy eagle is the world's most powerful eagle, able to hunt surprisingly large prey, from monkeys to sloths. These eagles have relatively short, broad wings and long tails that enable them to maneuver and hunt well in the forest. However, they can't manage the long, soaring flights of the more famous golden eagles and bald eagles of North America. Harpy eagles have impressive crests of long black plumes and enormous feet, the largest of any bird of prey. The foot of a harpy eagle is larger than most human hands.

Using these tremendous weapons and their powerful legs, harpy eagles can capture a variety of prey, including monkeys, sloths, porcupines, opossums, and even other birds, such as parrots. Harpy eagles hunt through the **canopy** of the tropical forests in their native South and Central America, rarely venturing above the tree tops.

Their nests are built high up in the trees, usually around 200 feet (60 m) above the ground. From that height they can watch for prey movement in all directions. The nests are built of sturdy sticks, woven to form a platform 4 feet (1.2 m) across and 2 feet (.6 m) deep. It is believed that harpy eagles breed only every other year, partly because the fledging period lasts for months. During that time the young eaglets remain near the nest, loudly calling to their parents for food, until they learn to hunt on their own.

Harpy eagles are under pressure from the clearing of tropical forests for timber and agriculture. A related species, the New Guinea harpy eagle from the island nation of Papua New Guinea in the Pacific Ocean north of Australia, faces the same problems of deforestation.

Hawaiian Goose

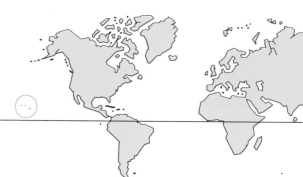

Nesochen sandvicensis

Range: Islands of Hawaii and Maui
Habitat: Sparsely vegetated volcanic slopes
Diet: Green vegetation and small berries
Size: 22–40 in. (56–100 cm) long
Reproduction: Average clutch: 4 eggs; incubation:
30 days
Threats Loss of habitat, predation, and low reproduction

The Hawaiian, or "ne ne," goose is the state bird of Hawaii. Its plumage is gray, brown, black and white. It has a distinctive, ivory-colored neck and a black head, beak, and tail. It lives on the islands of Maui and Hawaii in habitat consisting of upland slopes, above 5,000 feet (1,500 m), with scrubland and grasses and surrounded by rugged lava flows. Unlike most other geese, the Hawaiian goose does not require open water in which to feed. Instead, it feasts on native berries and green vegetation.

Hawaiian geese nest between October and February, returning to the same nesting area year after year. The female lays a clutch of from one to six eggs, which are incubated for a month. Goslings are flightless and must be closely protected by their parents, as they are very vulnerable to predation for the first three months.

At one time, before European settlers reached Hawaii, it was estimated that there were about 25,000 Hawaiian geese. Unfortunately, the species was an easy victim of overhunting and egg collecting, and by the early 1950s there were only 30 birds left. Captive breeding efforts have been very successful, and thousands of geese have been released. However, not all of these geese survive, and the consistent wild population remains at only around 400 birds. Limited habitat and scarcity of native food plants are thought to be the factors that keep the species population at this level.

Kirtland's Warbler

Dendroica kirtlandii

Range: North central Michigan; winters in the Bahamas
Habitat: Thickets of young jack pine
Diet: Insects, tree sap, and berries
Size: 6 in. (15 cm) long
Reproduction: Average clutch: 4–5 eggs; incubation: 14–15 days
Threats: Habitat loss, social parasitism by cowbirds

This tiny songbird is sometimes called "the bird of fire" because of its preferred nesting site: thickets of young jack pine trees. These trees grow only in the pine forests that spring up in areas that have been cleared by forest fires. This bird is blue-gray above and yellow with dark spots below. The Kirtland's warbler uses bark, grass, and pine needles to construct a nest on the ground, in which the female lays its eggs. Adults and nestlings feed on insects, which both parents catch to feed the **brood** until they fledge when four to five weeks old.

Breeding grounds are in north central Michigan, where the Kirtland's warbler spends late spring and summer before setting off on its annual migration to wintering grounds in the Bahamas and the Dominican Republic.

The principal reason the Kirtland's warbler is endangered is loss of habitat. The species needs a tract of jack pines of at least 80 acres (32 ha) and generally larger. However, in modern forest management, fires are often controlled and this has reduced the number of jack pine stands in Michigan. Today only about 4,500 acres (1,800 ha) of nesting habitat remain. Conservation efforts now include setting controlled forest fires within the Kirtland's warbler's native range. It is hoped that through this effort, and the planting of additional jack pines, the population will begin to grow.

Kirtland's warblers are also threatened by the increasing numbers of cowbirds within their range. Cowbirds are social parasites, laying their eggs in the nests of other birds, including Kirtland's warblers. The cowbird's eggs hatch before the warbler's, and the young are larger, so they get most of the food brought to the nest. The result is that fewer warblers survive. Today the U.S. Fish and Wildlife Service is working to reduce the number of cowbirds, as well as predators such as blue jays, from the Kirtland's warbler's range.

Masked Bobwhite

Colinus virginianus ridgwayi

Range: South central Arizona and northern Mexico
Habitat: Semiarid and desert grasslands
Diet: Seeds, plants, and insects
Size: 8–11 in. (20–27 cm) long
Reproduction: Clutch: 5–16 eggs; incubation: 23–24 days
Threats: Livestock grazing, fire suppression, predators

The masked bobwhite is a small quail species most famous for its call, the loud "bob-whoit" of the male. Like other quail, the masked bobwhite lives part of the year in social groups called coveys. These groups of up to 20 birds form during winter months and last until June, when the covey breaks up into breeding pairs.

The bird's mating and nesting depend directly on the summer rains in the desert region of southern Arizona and parts of northern Mexico where the species lives. Nesting on the ground, the bobwhite needs thick plant cover to conceal its clutch of eggs. If July rains are inadequate and the plants do not grow, the birds may not nest that year.

The masked bobwhite is endangered because its semiarid habitat has been altered by grazing cattle. The cattle eat all the grass, leaving the bobwhites without food or shelter. By 1900 the species was completely gone from Arizona, and numbers were dropping in Mexico as well.

Since the 1930s efforts have been made to reestablish masked bobwhites in their native range, using captive-bred birds. Early on, unfortunately, most of the released birds fell prey to coyotes. However, in 1985 the U.S. Fish and Wildlife Service protected an area of bobwhite habitat known as the Buenos Aires National Wildlife Refuge in the Alter Valley region of southern Arizona. Scientists now release captive-bred masked bobwhites in small family groups, together with wild-caught Texas bobwhites (a similar subspecies of quail) as foster parents to teach them survival skills.

Mauritius Kestrel

Falco punctatus

Range: The island of Mauritius
Habitat: Forest edges
Diet: Insects and small rodents
Size: 7–9 in. (17.5–22.5 cm) long
Reproduction: Average clutch: 2–3 eggs; incubation: 28 days
Threats: Clearing of habitat for sugar plantations and the subsequent insecticide spraying

In the 1970s the Mauritius kestrel was the most endangered bird of prey in the world, with only four birds surviving in the forests of the Black River Gorges on the island of Mauritius in the Indian Ocean.

This small falcon feeds on insects and small rodents. A clutch of two or three eggs is laid once a year in the hollow of a tree. Incubation takes about a month and is performed primarily by the female.

By 1992 the number of Mauritius kestrels in the wild was up to more than 170 birds, living in four separate forested areas. This dramatic increase was achieved by captive breeding and release of the birds in the wild, along with removal of some of the eggs from the nests of wild kestrels. Scientists in Mauritius discovered that if they removed the eggs from a wild nest shortly after they were laid, the female would soon lay another clutch. The first clutch could be incubated in captivity; either by a **surrogate** bird-parent, or in a mechanical incubator.

This "hands-on" approach to conservation was essential to increase the numbers of the species quickly. Since almost all the native forests on Mauritius had been cleared, the scientists decided to release the young kestrels into previously unused habitats. The birds adapted to new vegetation and agricultural areas and survived. Thus the Mauritius kestrel's range has been enlarged beyond the Black River Gorges region.

The goal of these conservation efforts is to have a healthy breeding population of more than 100 nesting pairs within the next few years.

Micronesian Kingfisher

Halcyon cinnamomina

Range: Native to Guam, extinct in the wild
Habitat: Stream banks and forest edges
Diet: Lizards, insects, amphibians, and fish
Size: 9 in. (22.5 cm) long
Reproduction: Average clutch: 1–4 eggs
Threats: Introduced predator

The Micronesian kingfisher is a beautiful little bird that resembles our native belted kingfisher in shape but is about half the size. Its long, daggerlike bill is used to capture prey, including reptiles, amphibians, insects, and small fish. The species is seen in forest areas along waterways, perching in trees and bushes before swooping down to catch its prey. The bird then typically returns to its perch to eat its catch.

The Micronesian kingfisher tunnels into mud banks, where it excavates a nest in which the female lays its clutch. Both parents help in incubating and feeding until the young fledge, after about three to four weeks.

The Micronesian kingfisher is the rarest of the 86 kingfisher species; so rare, in fact, that it no longer lives in the wild at all. It is native to the island of Guam, the largest of the Mariana Islands which stretch between New Guinea and Japan. However, today the species is extinct in the wild due to the accidental introduction of the poisonous brown tree snake in the 1940s.

Once it was discovered that the bird's numbers were critically low, Guam's Division of Aquatic and Wildlife Resources joined with several American zoos to try to save the kingfisher. They formed the Guam Bird Rescue Project to coordinate captive breeding of the Micronesian kingfisher and of the Guam rail. They hope, eventually, to reestablish the birds in their native habitat on the island of Guam.

Northern Spotted Owl

Strix occidentalis

Range: Pacific Northwest United States
Habitat: Old-growth coniferous forests
Diet: Small rodents, birds, reptiles, and insects
Size: 16–19 in. (40–47.5 cm) long
Reproduction: Average clutch: 1–2 eggs; incubation: 28–32 days
Threats: Clear-cutting in the old-growth forests of the Pacific Northwest

In the early 1990s the Northern spotted owl became a symbol of the struggle to save endangered species. This bird's native habitat is the old-growth forests of the U.S. Pacific Northwest. But the thickly wooded canyons and several-thousand-year-old conifer trees of these forests also attract timber companies.

The spotted owl is a large, dark-eyed **raptor** with white spots on its head. It is smaller than the more common barred owl but similar in markings. It is strictly nocturnal, feeding principally on rodents, birds, reptiles, and insects. It regularly caches, or hides, excess food to save for future need.

The species does not build nests; instead the birds simply scrape out a depression in debris on a cliff site or use an abandoned hawk nest. The female lays a clutch of 2-inch (5-cm)-long eggs, incubates the eggs, and remains with the young, being fed by the male until the owlets are about two weeks old. Pairs do not breed every year, but tend to return to the same nesting site when they do.

There is controversy over saving the spotted owls and the ancient forests where they live. Each pair of owls requires 1,400 to 4,500 acres (560–1,820 ha) for their home range. A stand of 100 acres (40 ha) of Douglas fir in Oregon is worth well over $2,000,000 today, and the timber industry provides jobs for many people. Therefore, some people say that it is too costly to protect this bird. But just as the whaling industry of a century ago has changed, forestry practices are also evolving, and the need for clearing the last of the giant trees of North America no longer exists.

Peregrine Falcon

Falco peregrinus

Range: All continents, except Antarctica, and many oceanic islands
Habitat: Nests on cliffs and buildings
Diet: Birds
Size: 15–20 in. (37.5–50 cm) long
Reproduction: Average clutch: 3–4 eggs; incubation: 29–32 days
Threats: Pesticides and pollution

The peregrine falcon is famous for capturing other birds in flight, for being the fastest bird in the world, and able to dive through the air at over 200 miles (320 m) an hour. It is a medium-size raptor with powerful, pointed wings, a narrow tail, and very large feet that it uses for catching birds on the wing. The falcon preys on a wide variety of birds, from blue jays and cuckoos to ducks, swooping down to attack its victims in a high-speed dive.

Peregrines do not construct nests but instead lay their clutch of eggs on rocky cliffs. Egg laying occurs in April and May, and both parents share incubation for about a month. Young peregrines are able to fly by early summer and remain with their parents until the fall migration. They do not breed until three years of age.

The peregrine has a broad distribution, with different subspecies ranging throughout much of the world. In the United States today, scientists estimate that there are 100 breeding pairs east of the Mississippi River and 400 pairs in the western part of the country. These numbers are up from a low in the 1970s when the peregrine was extinct in its eastern United States breeding range.

Peregrines are fast, but they are not fast enough to outfly pollution. The use of the deadly pesticide DDT in the 1950s and 1960s severely threatened this bird. The poison built up in the peregrines' bodies and led to a thinning of their eggshells, making them unable to produce young. However, the banning of DDT in 1972 and the introduction of captive-bred peregrines have helped bring back this species from the edge of extinction.

Although the peregrine falcon is a conservation success story, scientists are concerned about current pollutants, such as PCBs, that can also cause eggshell thinning.

Philippine Eagle

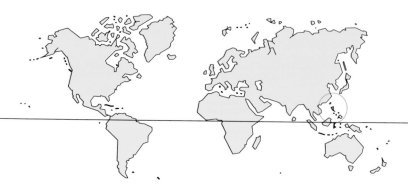

Pithecophaga jefferyi

Range: The Philippine Islands
Habitat: Tropical forests
Diet: Flying lemurs, other mammals, reptiles, and birds
Size: 43–48 in. (107.5–120 cm) long
Reproduction: Average clutch: 2 eggs
Threats: Extensive clear-cutting of forest habitat, human encroachment

The Philippine eagle is one of the largest raptors in the world. It is not quite as heavy as the harpy eagle or Steller's sea eagle, but it is a longer bird with a greater wingspan. Built something like a long-limbed basketball player, the Philippine eagle is surprisingly agile when it flies above the trees to defend its territory or to pursue prey. The species is perhaps best known for the circle of spiky neck and crest plumes, which give the bird a dramatic appearance.

Once called the "monkey-eating eagle," the Philippine eagle, in fact, eats more than just primates. Its diet includes flying lemurs, bats, other small mammals, snakes, and even birds, such as hornbills.

Philippine eagles build their nests high in trees, often as much as 200 feet (60 m) above the ground. The nest is constructed of sturdy sticks, which both parents bring to the site. Like most eagles, the Philippine eagle returns to the same nest for years, adding sticks each breeding season. Typical clutch is two, and the young are raised by both parents. Young eaglets stay with their parents for a period of months before heading out to establish their own territories.

Today it is estimated that only 300 to 500 Philippine eagles survive. Forest clearing and human population growth in the Philippine Islands have placed great pressure on these magnificent birds, although efforts are underway to protect remaining eagle habitat in the Philippine National Parks.

Piping Plover

Charadrius melodus

Range: Atlantic and Gulf coasts, Great Lakes, and Great Plains
Habitat: Beaches and sand bars
Diet: Marine crustaceans, shellfish, insects, and eggs of marine invertebrates
Size: 6–8 in. (15–20 cm) long
Reproduction: Average clutch: 4 eggs; incubation: 25–31 days
Threats: Habitat disturbance and coastal development

The piping plover is a small, short-billed shorebird with tan and white plumage that helps it blend in with its sandy habitat. Male and female piping plovers are similar in size and color. The species gets its name from its "piping" calls. The preferred diet is made up of small marine invertebrates, including crabs and mollusks.

Breeding season for the piping plover varies through its range but occurs during the spring or summer. After mating, the female and male plover together dig a simple cavity in the sand above high tide, where the female then lays a clutch of small, spotted, white eggs. The parents take turns incubating the eggs for about a month. After hatching, the young plovers are up and about, in search of food, within a few hours. The young stay with their parents for another month until they are ready to set out on their own.

The principal range of the piping plover is the mid-Atlantic coast of the United States, where an estimated 500 pairs nest each year. Smaller populations live in the Great Lakes and northern Great Plains regions.

The problem for piping plovers is that everybody likes to go to the beach. Unfortunately, that's where this species nests. To survive, the piping plover needs a stretch of undisturbed beach—something that is hard to find. Coastal development has destroyed plover habitat, and dune buggies and other vehicles destroy the bird's nests. Fortunately, wildlife managers and concerned citizens are working to fence off the beaches during the piping plover's nesting season. Successful efforts along the coast of Connecticut have led to the reestablishment of this species, and now more plovers are nesting there than in the past thirty years.

Quetzal

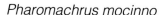

Pharomachrus mocinno

Range: Southern Mexico to Panama
Habitat: Tropical forests
Diet: Fruit
Size: 14–15 in. (35–37.5 cm) long; males have 24-in. (60-cm) tail feathers.
Reproduction: Average clutch: 2 eggs; incubation: 17–18 days
Threats: Deforestation

Birds are among the most brilliantly colored of all animals, and some species even have patches of iridescent feathers. But the resplendent quetzal seems to glow from head to tail. With emerald green plumage above, and a crimson belly, it is often thought to be the most beautiful animal in the world. The bird is about 15 inches tall, but the male's tail feathers can reach lengths of more than 24 inches.

The quetzal ranges in tropical cloud forest areas from southern Mexico and south through Central America to western Panama. During its elaborate courtship, the male quetzal repeatedly circles high above the trees, then drops down rapidly through the treetops while making a distinctive "wac-wac" sound. Males and females together build a nest in a hollowed-out hole in a rotting tree, then incubate the eggs and feed the young until they fledge, about 30 days after hatching.

Quetzals are principally fruit eaters, and are particularly fond of wild avocado fruit, from a tree in the laurel family. The birds swallow the small fruits whole, digest the fleshy part and regurgitate the seeds. The seeds sprout and take root on the forest floor. So the quetzal serves as an important seed disperser for this plant species.

The quetzal has been among the most prized birds in all history, yet hunting has not been the biggest threat. More than 1,000 years ago local peoples, including the Maya and Aztec Indians of Central America, protected the species. In Guatemala, the basic unit of money is called the quetzal in honor of the bird. It is protected by law in Costa Rica, where one of the largest populations remains. Unfortunately, the clearing of tropical forests in Central America makes it impossible for the quetzal to thrive. As the trees disappear, so will the beautiful quetzals.

Shoebill Stork

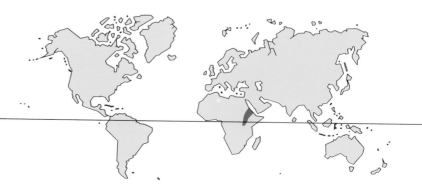

Balaeniceps rex

Range: Central and east Africa
Habitat: Papyrus and reed swamps
Diet: Fish, especially lungfish, baby crocodiles, water snakes, and small turtles
Size: 40–48 in. (100–120 cm) long
Reproduction: Average clutch: 2 eggs; incubation: 40 days
Threats: Limited habitat due to wetland drainage for irrigation

The shoebill stork is a 4-foot (1.2-m)-tall wading bird that is well adapted for life in the papyrus swamps of east Africa. Its name comes from its large bill, which it uses to reach through the matted reeds to catch fish. It is also called the whale-headed stork.

The shoebill stork may look clumsy because of its height, long legs, large feet, and huge bill, which it usually tucks down toward its breast. However, the bird is an agile flyer, sometimes using updrafts for gliding. Its oversize feet help the bird to walk on the matted reeds without sinking.

The bird's nest is a platform made up of water plants, where the female lays a clutch of eggs which incubate for about 40 days.

Favorite foods include lungfish, frogs, young turtles, and even small mammals and birds. When feeding, the bird stands with its bill pointed down and its neck and wings outstretched. Then it lunges downward, using its oversized bill to push through the matted papyrus to grab its prey.

Like many birds that can live only in specific habitats, the shoebill stork is shrinking quickly in numbers. While the species is not persecuted directly by humans, the drainage of wetlands and disturbance by cattle and people have caused its numbers to decrease drastically. It is thought that only 1,000 to 2,000 shoebills remain in the African wild.

Snail Kite

Rostrhamus sociabilis

Range: Everglades, southern Florida, Cuba, southern Mexico, South America
Habitat: Subtropical freshwater marshes
Diet: Apple snails
Size: 17–19 in. (42.5–47.5 cm) long
Reproduction: Average clutch: 3 eggs; incubation: 26–30 days
Threats: Loss of wetlands due to drainage and development

The snail kite gets its name from the fact that it specializes in eating one thing: apple snails. Its sharply curved bill is well adapted for pulling the snails from their shells. The species was formerly called the Everglades kite, for the Everglades region in Florida where it was often seen. However, it is also commonly found in wetlands in parts of Central and South America.

Snail kites are medium-size hawks with a wingspan of nearly 4 feet (1.2 m). Its hooked bill, and a white rump patch are its most distinguishing physical characteristic. During nesting season, the legs of the male turn bright orange-red. The kite once ranged through most of Florida but its numbers have declined drastically in recent years because of growing human demands for fresh water. When people use more and more water, less remains in wild areas. The apple snail—the snail kite's only food—lives in shallow, fresh water; and the snail kite cannot live without apple snails. In the early 1990s ornithologists—as scientists who study birds are called—estimated the snail kite's Florida population at 400 to 500 birds.

Conservationists are working to rescue the snail kite. Two important areas of kite habitat are being saved: 28,000 acres (11,200 ha) on the western shore of Lake Okeechobee and a 100-square-mile (260-sq-km) tract in southern Florida are the most important refuges. These areas don't save just kites; they are also home to thousands of other species, from bald eagles to indigo snakes and even apple snails.

Thick-Billed Parrot

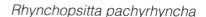

Rhynchopsitta pachyrhyncha

Range: Southern Arizona and northern Mexico
Habitat: Conifer and mixed deciduous forests
Diet: Conifer cones, acorns, juniper berries
Size: 16 in. (40 cm) long
Reproduction: Little is known about the thick-bill's nesting habits
Threats: Low numbers, collectors, habitat destruction

The thick-billed parrot is a medium-size green bird with red patches on its head, and a thick black bill. It is about 16 inches (40 cm) in length with a wingspan of 8 to 10 inches (20–25 cm). It is the only parrot species that nests in the United States today.

This parrot species prefers living in mountainous habitat, at elevations between 6,000 and 10,000 feet (180–300 m). Its principal foods are cones from evergreen trees, such as pines, firs, and spruce. It uses its curved bill to pull out seeds from the cones, but it also eats acorns from oak trees at lower elevations.

Like most parrots, the thick-billed parrot nests inside holes in trees. Since it is a small bird, it does not need a large hole and typically uses natural tree cavities or holes abandoned by woodpeckers.

The thick-billed parrot is native to Mexico and southern Arizona. It is endangered throughout its range because of pressure from human population growth and land development but is especially low in numbers in the United States. A flock of a dozen birds was reestablished in the Coronado National Forest in southeastern Arizona in the mid-1980s. Birds are added to this flock each spring, but the population has remained at about a dozen due to predation by goshawks, a bird-eating raptor species. However, young parrots have been spotted in Arizona, leading scientists to believe the birds are successfully breeding in the wild. The flock migrates north each summer to the Mogollon Rim in central Arizona.

Waldrapp Ibis

Geronticus eremita

Range: Southern Europe, northwestern Africa, and the Middle East
Habitat: Dry, open scrubland
Diet: Insects, small birds, mammals, and reptiles
Size: 28 in. (70 cm) long
Reproduction: Average clutch: 3–4 eggs; incubation: 4 weeks
Threats: Pesticides, habitat encroachment

The Waldrapp ibis, also known as the "bald ibis" and the "forest raven," is an unusual-looking bird with no facial or crown feathers. The feathers on the nape of its neck form a distinctive tuft. It is a relatively large bird, 28 inches (70 cm) in length, and most recognizable by the curved bill that is shared by all ibises.

The Waldrapp ibis nests in large colonies on high cliffs, laying three or four eggs each year. Incubation lasts four weeks, and the young remain in the nest for another seven weeks. Both parents share in the rearing of the young. Adult birds have dark, blackish plumage with red heads and legs; the young are an overall bronze color for the first year.

Active by day, they feed primarily on insects but also eat small birds, mammals, and reptiles.

This ibis once ranged in arid mountainous regions from southern Europe to northwestern Africa and the Middle East. Today, however, it is an extremely rare species, extinct throughout nearly all of its range. The bird's steady decline is the result of pesticide use, loss of feeding grounds, and human encroachment. Today it is being bred in zoos, with the hope of keeping the species alive. Plans are being made to release experimental colonies of captive-bred ibises within protected areas in their former range.

Whooping Crane

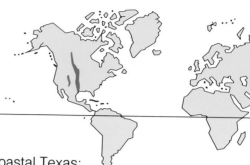

Grus americana

Range: Migrates from northern Canada to coastal Texas; experimental flock migrates from Idaho to New Mexico
Habitat: Wilderness wetlands and prairie pools
Diet: Crabs, clams, insects, small vertebrates, berries, and grains
Size: 50–54 in. (125–135 cm) long
Reproduction: Clutch: 2 eggs; incubation: 29–31 days
Threats: Shrinking habitat, small population in only two flocks

Whooping cranes are tall, long-legged white birds with black wing tips and red crowns on the tops of their heads. At 4.5 feet (1.35 m), they are the tallest birds in North America. They live in marshes and wetlands and, with their long legs, can wade into the water in search of small crabs and clams, which they swallow whole.

Like all cranes, whooping cranes mate for life. Every spring they go through elaborate courtship rituals that include dancing displays and loud singing calls. In late April the females lay two eggs. The crane pair then share in incubating and rearing their young.

Every year whooping cranes migrate thousands of miles from breeding grounds in Wood Buffalo National Park in central Canada to wintering grounds on Aransas Island National Wildlife Refuge, off the coast of Texas. Spring migration north is from late February through late April; fall migration south is from mid-September through mid-November.

Whooping cranes are staging a comeback. More whooping cranes are alive in the wild today than on the day you were born. From fewer than two dozen whooping cranes in the late 1960s, more than 300 "whoopers" are alive today.

Most of these cranes live in the flock that migrates from Canada to Texas each year. An experimental flock was also established by placing whooping crane eggs in the nests of sandhill cranes, which serve as surrogate parents. This flock of about two dozen birds migrates, along with the sandhill cranes, from Gray's Lake National Wildlife Refuge in Idaho, to Bosque del Apache National Wildlife Refuge in New Mexico, and back, each year.

Wood Stork

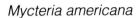

Mycteria americana

Range: Atlantic coast of United States, from South Carolina to Florida, south to Argentina
Habitat: Wetlands
Diet: Fish, amphibians, and aquatic invertebrates
Size: 34–47 in. (85–117.5 cm) long
Reproduction: Average clutch: 2–3 eggs; incubation: 28–32 days
Threats: Wetland destruction and habitat alteration

Wood storks are large white wading birds with bald heads and black flight feathers on the tips of their wings. Their thick, curved bills and long, thin legs allow them to probe shallow water for small fish and amphibians. Their wingspan is over 5 feet (1.5 m).

Cypress trees are the storks' preferred nesting sites, and 25 pairs may nest in the top of a tree at one time. These communal nesting sites are called **rookeries**. Although wood storks return to the same nest site year after year, their nests consist only of loose platforms of sticks and twigs on which the eggs are laid each spring.

About 60,000 wood storks were living in the southeastern United States in 1930. Today the National Audubon Society estimates that the population is one-fifth that size, about 12,000 birds.

The problem for wood storks is the decrease of wetland areas. Even in protected areas, such as Everglades National Park, nearby construction of canals and housing developments changes water levels and affects the bird's ability to hunt. In some cases the water has dried up under their rookeries. Raccoons then raid the wood stork nests at night and eat all the eggs.

Conservation sometimes calls for creative solutions and cooperation. In the mid-1980s, runoff from the Savannah River nuclear power plant was raising water levels to the point where wood storks were unable to feed. To save the wood storks, the U.S. Department of Energy worked with the Audubon Society, the U.S. Fish and Wildlife Service, and a local contractor to create a shallow lake in a dry lake bed. Now nearly 100 wood storks from the surrounding area will have foraging waters for years to come.

Many other birds are in danger throughout the world, including the three shown below. Our work is to save space on Earth for these and all other wild species.

Bali Mynah
Leucospar rothschildi

Range: Bali, Indonesia
Habitat: Tropical forest
Diet: Fruit and insects
Size: 10–11 in. (25–27.5 cm) long
Reproduction: Average clutch: 2–4 eggs; incubation: 3 weeks
Threats: Habitat destruction and the pet trade

Least Tern
Sterna antillarum

Range: Coastal United States and interior river systems
Habitat: Open sandy areas along shores
Diet: Fish, aquatic invertebrates
Size: 8–9 in. (20–22.5 cm) long
Reproduction: Average clutch: 2–3 eggs; incubation: 20 days
Threats: Channelization, river damage, disruption of nesting sites, predation

Red-Cockaded Woodpecker
Picoides borealis

Range: Southeast United States
Habitat: Old-growth pine stands and open pine woodlands
Diet: Wood-boring insects
Size: 8–9 in. (20–22.5 cm) long
Reproduction: Average clutch: 2–5 eggs; incubation: 10–15 days
Threats: Habitat destruction

Glossary

altricial   young that stay in the nest until they are nearly full-grown

arid   dry, desertlike conditions; of a habitat with low rainfall and sparse vegetation

brood   offspring born and raised together

canopy   the fairly continuous branch and leaf layer at the top of a forest, created by the intertwining of the tops of trees.

captive propagation   breeding in captivity, often as an attempt to increase the population of a species critically low in number

carrion   dead animals eaten by vultures and other scavengers

clutch   the number of eggs laid in one breeding

courtship   behavior in animals prior to mating

DDT   a hydrocarbon-based pesticide that causes eggshell thinning in birds.

fledge   the stage of development when young birds are fully feathered and leave the nest

incubation   keeping eggs warm until they hatch

larvae   a stage in the metamorphosis of some invertebrates in which the preadult form does not resemble the adult; beetle grubs and moth caterpillars are larvae.

migration   annual movement of a species due to changes in food availability and climate

raptor   a bird of prey; raptors include hawks, eagles, owls, and vultures

rookery   the communal nesting site of birds that nest together

subspecies   a group that can be distinguished physically from other members of the species

surrogate   a substitute; in breeding, an individual that serves as a foster parent

talons   the sharp claws on the feet of birds of prey

territory   the area an animals lives in and will defend against intruders

wetlands   wet, marshlike areas that have at least some surface water during all or part of the year

Bird and Wildlife Conservation Organizations

Cape May Bird Observatory
East Lake Dr.
Cape May Point, NJ 08212

Conservation International
1015 18th St. NW
Washington, DC 20036

Ducks Unlimited
1 Waterfowl Way
Memphis, TN 38120

Hawk Mountain Sanctuary Association
Route 2, Box 191
Kempton, PA 19529

International Council for Bird Preservation
32 Cambridge Rd.
Girton, Cambridge
England CB3 OPJ

International Crane Foundation
Shady Lane Rd.
Baraboo, WI 53913

National Audubon Society
950 Third Ave.
New York, NY 10022

National Wildlife Federation
1400 16th St., NW
Washington, DC 20036

The Nature Conservancy
1815 N. Lynn St.
Arlington, VA 22209

The Peregrine Fund
5666 West Flying Hawk La.
Boise, ID 83709

Wildlife Conservation International
New York Zoological Society
185th St. & Southern Blvd.
Bronx, NY 10460

World Wildlife Fund
1250 24th St., NW
Washington, DC 20037

For Further Reading

Bruchac, Joseph, and Michael Caduto. *Keepers of the Earth*. Golden, CO.: Fulcrum, 1989.

Burton, Philip. *Vanishing Eagles*. New York: Dodd, Mead, 1983.

Dobkin, David, and Paul Ehrlich, eds. *The Birder's Handbook: A Field Guide to the Natural History of North American Birds*. New York: Simon & Schuster, 1988.

Matthews, John R., and Charles J. Moseley, eds. *The Official World Wildlife Fund Guide to Endangered Species of North America*. Washington, D.C.: Beacham, 1990.

Parnall, Peter. *The Daywatchers*. New York: Macmillan, 1984.

Parnall, Peter. *The Nightwatchers*. New York: Macmillan, 1985.

PERIODICALS

Audubon magazine

International Wildlife magazine

National Wildlife magazine

Wildlife Conservation magazine

ZOOBOOKS, 930 W. Washington Street, San Diego, CA 92103 (published monthly)

Index

Northern Spotted Owl

Red-cockaded Woodpecker

Bald Eagle

Kirtland's Warbler

Least Tern

Whooping Crane

Hawaiian Goose

North America

California Condor

South America

Masked Bobwhite

Attwater's Prairie Chicken
Brown Pelican

Thick-billed Parrot

Piping Plover

Quetza